Mindful
Leadership

Mindful
Matters!

Holly Duckworth
2019

Mindful
Leadership

THE

TO

Guide for Stress-Free Leadership

Holly Duckworth

IonePublishing

Mindful Leadership: The A to Z Guide For Stress-Free Leadership
Published by Ione Publishing
Denver, CO

Library of Congress Control Number: 2018902716

ISBN-13: 978-1-7320198-1-2

Leadership & Management / Self Help / Mindfulness

QUANTITY PURCHASES: Schools, companies, professional groups,
clubs, and other organizations may qualify for special terms when
ordering quantities of this title. For information, email holly@
hollyduckworth.com

Introduction

Leading today is hard. It takes a new level of fortitude, and a bit of faith. Our world is in need of mindful leaders, and yet few people even know what mindfulness is.

Mindfulness — the practice of becoming fully present in the current moment.
Mindfulness is not meditation.
Mindfulness is not yoga.
While mindfulness can be practiced with meditation and yoga that is not the only way to become mindful.
Mindfulness does not require you to sit on a meditation pillow or wake up early.
Mindfulness is not about being perfect; it's about the practice.

This book gives you the information and practices to be mindfully centered in your body and mind in every experience you lead today.

The choice to explore these practices and lead mindfully invites men and women from all walks of life, and all faith paths, to be authentic and highly successful.

Why now?

The world today is as confusing as it is stressful. The stress we are putting on ourselves and leadership is unsustainable. Heart attack rates in this country are skyrocketing, diabetes, obesity, suicide, and divorce are all running rampant.

Organizations struggle to find people willing to step up and lead.

What is this book?

This book is infotainment. Here you will find information on mindfulness and a meditative coloring book for those who choose to use it that way.

Who is this book for?

This book was written for people who see the trend in leadership, the trend back to a more human way of leading. Perhaps you have been a leader for your entire career and are experiencing the exhaustion of overwhelm, this book is for you. Or, you are the leader with an hour glass watching the sands of time slip past you each day, a little closer to retirement, this book will help you think leadership legacy. Maybe you are the leader new in your role and you want to build an organization that honors the work to be done, the vision to be created, but you are not willing to sell your soul to a company. This book is for you.

How to use this book:

Mindful Leadership: The A to Z Guide For Stress-Free Leadership is designed to be an informational and entertainment coloring book. This being an infotainment book, I would invite you to use the book in the way that you learn best. Some of you will simply enjoy looking at the mandala letters, activities and read it cover to cover. Others will choose to read a page and color in the mandalas while doing the journal practices. I recommend that you grab a journal and spend some time each day doing one of the practices in this book. Have fun, pull out the color crayons or colored pencils and explore how the coloring of each letter can relax you while taking you deeper into each of the concepts. There is no right or wrong way to flip thru the concepts and practices. Doing one practice a day for a month will allow you to fully take in the images, apply the practices and use them in your life. Mindfulness is the practice of being present in each moment. Be present with this book. This book is for the stress-free dreamer in you. Take a few moments each day to really take in each page and let it tell you the story it wants you to know.

A

Affirmation

An affirmation is a short, positive, present tense statement that captures what you truly want. Affirmations help mindful leaders to reframe their mind to be positive in every situation. When you write affirmations on areas that challenge you, statistics show, you can overcome those challenges faster.

Example: I am a powerful leader in all that I do.

Journal Practice

Write your affirmative statement and put it in a place where you will read it multiple times a day. I recommend your mirror, car and at your desk. Monitor how the affirmation begins to show up in your life.

Complete this affirmation:
I am...

_____

_____

_____

B

Believe

Beliefs are the conscious and unconscious thoughts that fuel our lives. If you look at the world carefully and re-arrange the letters you may even see BE-Live. Beliefs are the lenses that create our lives.

Example: I believe that the vision of my life can come true.

Journal Practice

Ask yourself the following question and answer from your heart – What do I believe about money? Examine your beliefs on money; relationship; education; career; health.

As you look at the answers ask yourself: "Are these truly the beliefs I want to have in each area?" If not, look at changing one area each month for the next few months. You will be amazed at how you can reimagine yourself from the place of belief.

If I believed all things were possible in my life I would…

_____

_____

_____

C

Center

The pace of life today is built so we will stay in motion. The faster we move the more we are rewarded. A mindful leader knows when to sit still. It is said: "Be still, and know." Centering is the process of bringing your awareness back into your body.

Example: When you have a many tasks coming your way that can be a reminder it is time to center. Many leaders I work with practice centering by stepping away from that meeting breathing, mindfully focusing on their feet on the ground and bringing their attention to the center of what they must focus on in that moment.

Journal Practice

Take a moment today to center into your breath. Take a moment to feel your heart in the center of you chest. Move your awareness there and see how you can make more calm decisions from a centered place.

Find a comfortable place to sit. Breathe and feel into your heart center.

_____

_____

_____

D

Desire

When was the last time you let yourself feel passionate and want of something more for yourself or your organization? This is desire. We live in a feeling Universe that is activated by our hearts desire. Just like you feel the sun on your skin on a warm day, you can feel the desire of something happening in your life and business.

Example: It is my deepest desire to complete this project at work with ease, joy and fun. I will benefit, as will our customers, and my company.

Journal Practice

Take a moment today and connect to your heart. What is it you truly, desire personally and professionally?

_____

_____

_____

E

Expand

Leading in any organization requires us to expand what we think is possible. Just like your heart expands and contracts, so do your lungs. When and where is it time for you to naturally expand as a leader?

Example: Humans have a natural expansion that happens as we grow. We expand thru school from elementary, middle, high school and beyond.

Journal Practice

How are you supposed to expand your work in the world?

_____

_____

_____

F

Flow

Rivers flow, clouds move, and winds blow – all the world around us is in a constant state of flow. You are one with that flow. Mindful leaders practice being in a state of flow with the work they do and the things they have to accomplish.

Example: As a leader, your day has a natural flow to each day, week and year. Pay attention to where the day naturally flows and where you find resistance.

Journal Practice

What is one area you need to let go of your need to control and simply flow with what the Universe is trying to bring you? Is it possible it could be better than what you are holding on to?

_____

_____

_____

G

Gratitude

In "B" we said it is done unto us, as we believe. Do you believe in the good that is all around you? When we sense the world is for us, we bring more of that good to our experience of life.

Example: When you are a generous giver with gratitude pay attention to how good is returned to you. Often when I find myself giving of my mentoring time to future leaders I find other leaders offering to support my work.

Journal Practice

What are 5 things you are grateful you had the opportunity to give today? Put some of your good out into the world today. Send a thank you note, buy someone's coffee, let a car in that's trying to crowd in at an intersection. Do more good! Good works!

_____

_____

_____

H

Hope

In turbulent times, it's important to remember the still small voice in you that hopes, dreams and visions.

Example: At times, leadership requires us to face challenging obstacles. Mindful leaders are able to see and feel a sense deep within them, and their team, that something good will follow the challenge.

Journal Practice

What do you hope will happen for you, your team and the work you do? Is there someone on your team that could use a little hope? Call them and help them write an affirmation to start feeing hope again.

_____

_____

_____

I

Intention

An intention is your energy in motion. In contrast to your "to do" list, intention is a starting point of a dream. It takes the ideas from your head and moves them to your heart.

Example: I intend to complete my company leadership development plan knowing my team is powerful, productive and profitable.

Journal Practice

What is one thing on your "bucket" list you have always wanted to do? Take it off that list and move it into your heart and set it in motion. What is one intention you have to be a mindful leader? Your intention aligns with the consciousness of the Universe to make it happen.

_____

_____

_____

J

Joy

At the pace of life today it is easy to feel busy, overwhelmed and fearful. It is just as easy to choose joy. A mindful leader chooses joy in their body ever day. Joy is happiness, delight, bliss. Joy is allowing yourself to feel happy even in a world that sometimes does not want you to feel happy.

Example: Find something that makes you joy filled and do more of it. Do you like having coffee with clients, walking the production floor, traveling, crafting? Do more of that. If you enjoy music, listen to more of it. When you are feeling joyful, you invite the flow of happiness into your life and your leadership.

Journal Practice

Make a list of 3 things that bring you joy. Now get out your calendar and schedule 3-30 minutes a week to be fully in that activity.

_____

_____

_____

K

Knowing

Within each of us is the ability to deeply know something. To have knowledge from your head is called wisdom. To have knowledge from your spirit, (or soul) this is called knowing.

Example: That moment when you just have an unexplainable knowing that are being guided in a different direction and you have a choice to follow it or not. If you act on that intuition or inner knowing with intent good things can come your way.

Journal Practice

As you approach your desk today take 3-5 minutes in the quiet and ask your inner spirit voice if there is anything it would like you to know today. Listen with a pen in hand and write down what it tells you. Make time to act on it.

_____

_____

_____

L

Love

In America we have a very limited definition of love as an experience often between two people. Love can be far more expansive than that. Love is why we are here, who we came here to be and what we came to give.

Example: Look at all the ways you get to love as leader. Start with yourself. Do you love yourself, how you show up being a leader? Look at how you love your team, clients and vendors. Love is a many splendored word. A mindful leader knows love fuels their success.

Journal Practice

What does love mean to you? How can you bring more love to the people you lead to be a more mindful leader?

_____

_____

_____

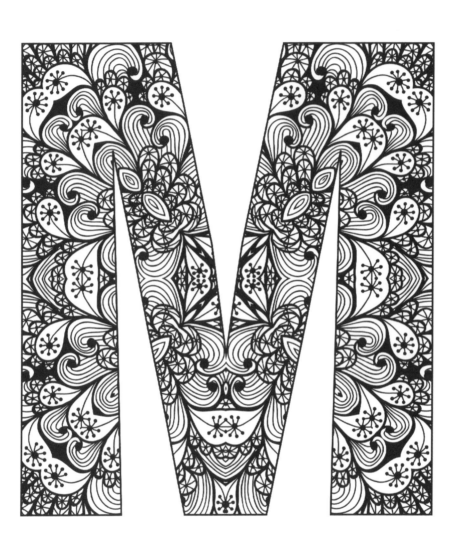

M

Movement & Meditation

Meditation is the ancient practice of going within to find your own inner wisdom. There are many ways to practice meditation. Not all of them require you to sit in the lotus position and focus on your breath. Mindful meditation is finding a way for you to connect to your own center and wisdom.

Example: Mindful meditation can happen in many ways. Try mindful eating by focusing on every aspect of eating from picking up the fork, taking a bite and swallowing. Mindful walking is another way to be fully present, feel your feet hit the ground with each step; feel your feet lift off the ground for each subsequent step.

Journal Practice

Find one way to move today and become fully present in that experience. Try walking, eating, driving, dancing any form of movement will work when you practice being fully present with that. Once you are completed journal how that experience felt in your body and mind.

_____

_____

_____

N

New Thoughts

Leaders often find a routine of being and do the "same old, same old" each day. Being a mindful leader in today's world requires us to have new thoughts. Your thoughts shape your world and the world you lead from. New Thoughts happen when you ask great questions.

Example: Here are a few questions that can open you to new conversations with yourself and your team.

Why am I engaging in the work I am doing?
How am I inviting my team to try something new and feel safe?
What is my mind to do on this project?

Journal Practice

What is one new thought you would like to have about your Leadership style?

_____

_____

_____

O

Openness

As the day in day out grind of leadership can sometimes happen we become numb, stagnant or still in the repetition of life. Openness is mindfully taking off any points of restriction in your thoughts, beliefs or actions. Become willing and open to have a new experience.

Example:
Open your hands wide and feel how they feel differently than when you have your hands on your computer keyboard, phone or other device. Open your hand wider — look at it and invite something new to open your hand, heart, mind and experience. The more we can keep the energy of our bodies' open the more new experiences can come in.

Journal Practice

If I were truly open to leading mindfully I would stop doing the following _____

_____

As I expand my openness I am letting more _____ into my life and I _____

_____

P

Possibilities

As a young child we often hear "no" more time than we hear "yes".
Now to be a mindful leader we must stay in the infinite possibilities.
Mindful leaders are possibility people.

Example: Your mindset sets your trajectory of what you think is
possible. If you think you can only have a little good, then only a
little you will have. It takes the same energy to have a little as a lot so
why not set the possibility to your maximum good.

Journal Practice

Use your "M" meditation practice (be that a movement or seated
meditation) and open your heart to see what new possibilities may be
wanting to emerge from your ability to now see them.

_____

_____

_____

Q

Questions in Quiet

As a leader we all have bought into a belief system that a leader must be available all the time. That is simply not only not true, it's not realistic.

Example: Our loud world can sometimes block or distract us from the mindful wisdom that wants to come thru us. Mindful leaders schedule personal time for reflection and rejuvenation. They know that when they take this time and make it a priority they inspire their leaders to do the same and everyone can lead from a healthier more mindful, centered place.

Journal Practice

Schedule 5-30 minutes of quite time for you each day. Keep track of the benefits you get from having this time each day.

_____

_____

_____

R

Release

Just like a glass cannot hold infinite liquid humans cannot hold infinite ideas and actions. We must let go of things that no longer support us doing our work leading in the world.

Example: Look at nature; it does not hold all the leaves all year long. The leaves come and go to support the trees. Employees do not come on your team and stay forever. They come to do the work that you need and the leave once their assignment is complete.

Journal Practice

Ask your mindful self what is it time for you to let go of so your leadership can expand even more good in the world?

_____

_____

_____

S

Spirit

One of the most mis-understood words in our language, spirit means many things to different people. Spirit is energy. Spirit is the composition of your character, emotions and soul. It is the alchemy of who you are being and becoming on this planet.

Example: Spirit is the essential energy that you are. Have you ever had the experience of walking up to someone and you feel/sense they are sad or depressed. You have this experience of them over and over. This is their Spirit.

Journal Practice

What is your Spirit? What energy do you give off each day? Take 5-10 minutes in the meditation practice of your choice to determine if your Spirit is what you want it to be in the world.

_____

_____

_____

T

Trust

I use this acronym for TRUST to help me think about defining what it means to trust:

Total **R**eliance on **U**niversal **S**ource **T**oday

Trust is a confidence you put in yourself and the persons, places and things around you.

Example: When you are driving you trust that the drivers in the other lanes will stay in their lane. When you visit a restaurant you trust that the chef will bring you healthy food. Your team trusts you as a mindful leader that you will give your best to the work you lead, and they give you that in return.

Journal Practice

What does trust mean to me? How do I build trust in myself as a leader and with my team?

_____

_____

_____

U

Unconditional

Becoming mindful is the art of setting an intention in motion and unconditionally breathing closer to the vision each day.

Journal Practice

Write a list of those things you truly love unconditionally. The people, places and things that have supported you in good times and bad.

_____

_____

_____

V

Visioning & Visualization

Visioning is the process of seeing something. For example if I say, see a beach at sunset, in your minds eye you will see a sandy beach with sky changing color. Visualization is the process of seeing that same beach only you see yourself on the beach.

Example: Vision boards. When you make a vision board and put it in a prominent location your mind keeps seeing the vision over and over and begins to work to make it a reality. Our brain and experience does not know the difference between imagined reality and actual reality. So the more you visualize the more you actualize.

Journal Practice

Ask your inner wisdom guide the following:
- What is the highest vision for this project?
- What must I let go of for this project to mindfully grow?
- What must I embrace to grow this project?
- What should I know at this time?

_____

_____

_____

W

Wander & Wonder

Not all who wander are lost. As mindful leadership practices grow in companies and as you practice mindfulness in your life it is valuable to wander a bit.

Example: The definition of insanity is doing the same thing over and over and expecting different results. Mindful leaders do different things over and over and anticipate different results. Allow yourself to wander as a leader and give your team permission to explore too. Your willingness to wonder will bring new solutions to you.

Journal Practice

Look around you today and look for something wonderful. Here's a hint: it may be up, down, to your left or to your right. Look in a new direction. Go explore and wander. Write your experiences here.

_____

_____

_____

X

eXcitement

As you practice mindfulness and put into practice the A to Z of mindful leadership, you will begin to uncover a sense of excitement. Excitement is a feeling of enthusiasm and joy.

Example: As you practice mindfulness in your words with new affirmations, with your new thoughts and questions and begin to believe differently about yourself and your team, you will have an enthusiasm about the great life you are creating for yourself and your company.

Journal Practice

I am excited that I have become _____ as a result of leading mindfully.

_____

_____

_____

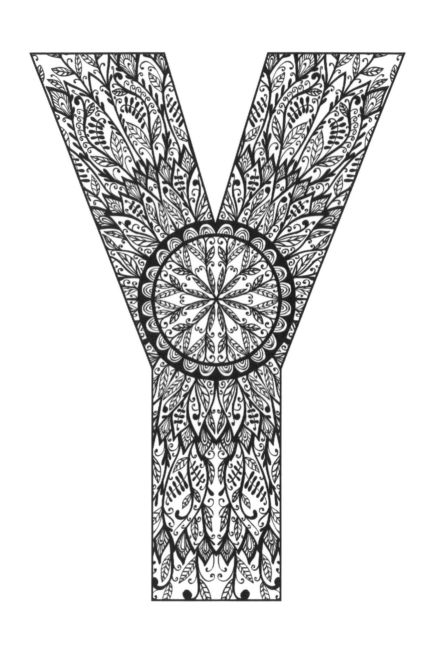

Y

Yes!

Living the A to Z practices in mindfully is a way to say "yes" to living life fully and authentically.

Example: What do you do when a new opportunity comes to you. Mindful leaders will center into the knowing and knowledge within them and make a decision from that place of trust.

Journal Practice

As you do your mindful practice today eating, walking driving, or journaling give some thought to what you are giving a big "yes" to. What do you affirm and what more do you want in your life.

_____

_____

_____

Z

Zeal & Zest

Practicing mindful leadership invites us to a new awareness of the energy around us. As a mindful person you then can practice using your energy in a positive way. When you are positive, your life becomes lighter and burdens seem to fall away.

Example: One of my coaching clients recently learned a big client was not renewing their contract resulting in devastating effects to their organization. As a result of his mindful practice this leader was able to center, focus on the vision he wanted and with zeal and zest open-up to new beginnings.

Journal Practice

What are you passionate about in leading because of these 26 mindful leadership practices, mindful meditative coloring, journaling and conversations?

_____

_____

_____

Thank you

THANK YOU FIRST TO YOU for being willing to explore leading differently in these challenging times. Thank you for purchasing this book exploring it's content and applying it's practices. You make our world a better place by being in it.

It takes a village to live mindfully. To find people who will support you in when your road goes dark and yet the spark within still burns brightly.

This year has been especially challenging as I have prepared new keynotes, columns, articles and this book. I would like to thank the following for their unconditional love.

- ⚗ My family, my parents Mike and Shirley, my sister Michele and her husband Rob. My brother Brian and his family Tiffanie, Brayden, Ella and Lukas your visit here to see me in Colorado meant so much.

- ⚗ My friends — Carolyn Strauss, Rochelle Rice, Christy Lamagna, Debby Schacht, Lori Anne Rising, Pegine Echevaria, John Chen, Nick Hemmert, Phil Gerbyshak, Eric Rozenberg, and Keith Renninson all of you have contributed calls, edits, smiles and words of encouragement when I wanted to stop producing this book.

  ⌘ My clients who have supported my journey of lifelong learning and practice of these principles day in and day out. You are always willing to listen to my crazy insights and apply them to your work.

  ⌘ My spiritual community — naming names is sure to mean I will forget someone, but here goes. First to my beloved prayer partner Georgena Eggleston who knows me, lives with me, laughs with me and cries at every fork in my path. To Michael Lang who reads everything I write before it goes to the public, Sharon Shores who was brave enough to say yes to mentor me as a practitioner. To Michelle Medrano, Roger & Erica Teel and the Board of Directors who keep the lighthouse burning. My colleagues and columnists at Science of Mind Magazine, David Goldberg & Holly Sharp who keep me looking sharp.

  ⌘ Steven & Karin Snyder thank you for inviting me to be your down stairs neighbor your support and encouragement made this book possible in ways no words can describe.

  ⌘ And lastly to Polly Letofsky and Andrea Costantine thank you for giving me the courage to put words on the page and making my words look great once I did.

About the Author

Holly Duckworth, CAE, CMP, LSP is a New York Times contributor on the topic of mindfulness. She is an award-winning author on volunteerism and association leadership. Holly is THE expert organizations worldwide go to for insights on how to stay in the present moment even in these challenging and uncertain times. She is high energy when you need a boost and a compassionate ear or when you just need someone to listen. She is the one to call when you are ready for positive energy and mindful change of leadership.

For more on keynote speaking, training or executive coaching with Holly Duckworth, CAE, CMP visit www.hollyduckworth.com or follow her on:

Linked In: www.linkedin.com/in/hduckworth/
Twitter: @hduckworth